more praise for

ALL OF US ARE CLEAVED

T0300783

"Within *All Of Us Are Cleaved* a language of love & forgiveness emerges from the mother wound & the deepest wound of colonization. The lyric of the word blooms within this collection of poems—as your body merges with the work you begin to understand the purpose of love. Here an intimacy of poetics—each poem moving through life as life naturally does through the personal to the outer that resembles all of us. Here we rest our cheek on each other's body, un abrazo fuerte enveloping each other—medicine that is a balm—like the Vicks rubbed on your chest cuando eramos niños—here a poetics of intimacy that equals the history of each others' flesh."

LOURDES FIGUEROA
author of the chapbook *Vuelta*

"As the contronym in the title suggests, Llagas's poems grapple with the inherent contradictions that complicate and enrich human existence, and signal the oppositions that can divide us should our vigilance in interrogating their historically-and culturally-constructed assumptions wane. These poems form a relentless investigation into the author's double heritages: first, as a first-generation Filipino immigrant raised during the Marcos dictatorship but later naturalized as an American citizen in adulthood, both unwilling product of empire and implicated agent of imperialism. Additionally, the poems probe the speaker's self-identities as a Catholic-raised practicing Buddhist, an educated and socially mobile working class-derived member of society, a woman protective of both her individuality and her recent marriage, and an introspective poet seeking concrete social change. Rather than goad us to take sides or force a reconciliation among such oppositions, Llagas's poems thrive at the intersections, revealing and enlarging the tensions among identities and allegiances, and in doing so create a new space – a more empathetic and giving space – for individual, interpersonal, and interrelational exchange. As the speaker tells the Covid pandemic in one poem: 'You rupture us whole.' Similarly, the deeply lyrical and meditative poems in this collection break wide open the cracks that delineate facile categorizations, and from these fissures form new openings from where to more deeply and more compassion-ately view the world."

ABIGAIL LICAD
poet, critic, and former editor-in-chief
for *Hyphen* magazine

"Karen Llagas' much-anticipated new collection is a fresh rendering of movement, memory, and lineation. Pay close attention to space and structure, to permeability and deliberate acts of grace. Just as there are many paths to excavating lost places and histories, the speaker in these poems takes us on an imagistic journey to rituals of grieving and cleaving (a 'thirst for salt and mud'), to fields of sugarcane and the many kinds of poverty and privilege, always in proximity to the smallest of bodies—bees, spiders, yeast, rice grains, origins. ('Do you know a rosebud/ that refuses/ to bloom is called a bullet?') These are, at once, field notes and love poems, unsentimental and unimpeachable."

AILEEN CASSINETTO
Academy of American Poets Laureate Fellow

NOMADIC PRESS

OAKLAND

PHILADELPHIA

XALAPA

WWW.NOMADICPRESS.ORG

Through publications, events, and active community participation, Nomadic Press collectively weaves together platforms for intentionally marginalized voices to take their rightful place within the world of the written and spoken word. Through our limited means, we are simply attempting to help right the centuries' old violence and silencing that should never have occurred in the first place and build alliances and community partnerships with others who share a collective vision for a future far better than today.

INVITATIONS Nomadic Press wholeheartedly accepts invitations to read your work during our open reading period every year. To learn more or to extend an invitation, please visit: www.nomadicpress.org/invitations

DISTRIBUTION
Orders by teachers, libraries, trade bookstores, or wholesalers:

Nomadic Press Distribution
orders@nomadicpress.org
(510) 500-5162

Small Press Distribution
spd@spdbooks.org
(510) 524-1668 / (800) 869-7553

MASTHEAD

FOUNDING PUBLISHER
J. K. Fowler

LEAD EDITOR
Karthik Sethuraman

ASSOCIATE EDITOR
Michaela Mullin

DESIGN
Jevohn Tyler Newsome

All of Us Are Cleaved
© 2022 by Karen Llagas

This book was made possible by a loving community of chosen family and friends, old and new. For author questions or to book a reading at your bookstore, university/school, or alternative establishment, please send an email to info@nomadicpress.org.

Cover art and author portrait by Arthur Johnstone

Published by Nomadic Press, 1941 Jackson Street, Suite 20, Oakland, CA 94612
First printing, 2022

Library of Congress Cataloging-in-Publication Data

Title: *All of Us Are Cleaved*
p. cm.
Summary: Karen Llagas's All of *Us Are Cleaved* explores how we are shaped by the connections we form and are thrusted upon us. From the intimate spaces of marriage and family to the wider experiences of migration, political engagement and a global pandemic, these poems assert that we are simultaneously taken apart and put back together: by our individual efforts, yes, but also by our collective grace.

[1. XX. 2. XX. 3. XX. 4. XX. 5. American General.]

LIBRARY OF CONGRESS CONTROL NUMBER: 2022947165
ISBN: 978-1-955239-43-1

ALL OF US ARE CLEAVED

ALL OF US ARE CLEAVED

POEMS BY KAREN LLAGAS

**NOMADIC
PRESS**

Oakland · Philadelphia · Xalapa

CONTENTS

introduction

reading guide

INTRODUCTION

Many years ago, in a talk about creative process, a writer said, "I write to see if I can believe what I feel." I often refer back to this scribbled quote in my notebook and have since arranged and re-arranged it whenever I needed to ground myself back on why I write: I write to see if I can trust what I have become. I write to see if I believe who I said I am. I write because I otherwise become only the identities I have taken on: a wife, a stepmom, a daughter, a sister & friend, a teacher, an ally, a first-generation immigrant, a person of color, a woman. Society often rewards us for being good at our roles. Yet how can I participate fully in the necessary work of healing without first enacting and re-enacting my freedom? And where would I start if not on the page that first called me home?

2020 was a difficult year, year of individual and collective losses for most if not all of us. It marked other events for me: it was the year that my total years in the U.S. surpassed my total years in the Philippines. This moment felt significant, clarifying for me that a historical self does not get "defined" as much as it gets "accumulated." It was also the year I last spent time with my grandmother in our hometown before she passed away at 91: she was a force and a source of intellectual engagement and community leadership for many, and for me, the first to encourage my love of books & learning, to model a tough mind and a soft heart.

If issues of language and memory persist in this collection, so do multiplicities. The stories and struggles of communities in the Philippines remain as alive and vibrant to me as those of my more immediate family and community here in California. If my poems were shaped by an early childhood spent under an oppressive dictatorship and by migration, they are also acutely aware of the privileged positions I occupy—that I could work with relative safety during the pandemic, for example, or that my husband and I have the resources to cultivate a garden, to take care of our beloved dogs.

Many poems here were written recently, shortly after the pandemic began in 2020. After years of not consistently writing or sending work out, I decided that I would place myself again "in the path" of poetry, to paraphrase another writer: to write, seek out and support other writers in various ways, to push up against a norm that insists, despite daily proof, that there's not enough generosity to go around. Many of the poems here reflect the emergency I felt, as well as the emergence that moves alongside it.

I hope I also wrote enough about joy and pleasure, about intimacy and about the ordinary days where I found refuge. This collection exists in big part because other poets have shown me what it means to reach across time and space to touch another person's life; to give and receive gifts of connection. If you're holding this chapbook, I hope the work converses with you. I hope a bit more light seeps into your day as you read through the poems.

SELF-PORTRAIT AS HEAP AND WILT,

as opposite of saint,   less field of ranunculus
                     and more nematodes
in the spill of spring,
the dirt the monk is scooping, more
                     than his calm,

the want to be the garden
               and finding
the slab of brick
                       and faucet shards
topped over by mulch. Not lavender

but snow-in-
summer groundcover,   the rust

that has leaked on grass,
neither metropolis nor old rural,

I am each radical,
             all chemical, open pit mining,
canaries that flew back.

GRATITUDE JOURNAL

I flinch as I reach for it, this practice
we do each night in bed,

our pillow talk these days,
when sending ourselves off to sleep

needs less effort than late night sex.
Does this flinch expose how little regard

I have for joy? Is this why I clasp our one-
dollar journal like an amulet? One time I wrote

oysters at the balcony, all
shucked by you.

Another day, *sleeping in*.
You always thank a task at work,

some beautiful fish or other.
Tonight is a small entry: the word *and*,

how I carry a small syllable
to bridge in me the scared

and sacred, to help me sing well enough
the everyday swirls

and chaos. Can I do one small
thing to further us along?

My early ancestors survived,
turning towards what

they destroyed. They killed
so much, now I don't have to,

at least not as much, especially
not myself, not the tenderest part.

ADULT SWIM CLASS

First we needed to unlearn a few things.
                              We needed to consider the water. Walking
   on land is to fall forward and catch ourselves

   again and over. The world was to stand upon,
            we found we couldn't effort
              our way to buoyant:
  we sink because
      we struggle, our efforts do not consider
                        the water. Also we've been told it doesn't happen

                        when one's old since we panic at the slightest
      out-of-breathness. The logic of water is of least
resistance: it flows and flows. No wonder the first

class is just to know in the body: to let go is to float
                        face up to the sky, skin barely breaking
                              surface, trusting the muscles to remember.

TAMAYO'S ANIMALES

Two dogs bark at a moon that mocks
the little it takes to give them pleasure.

Or, two dogs laugh at something as far
as the moon, at how little it takes
to give them pleasure.

Their eyes smolder chili and charcoal,
letting the world know

not *what* but *that* they want,
Here, in a newly risen world,
three polished, symmetrical bones—

because to be an animal is to glow with hunger
for what is discarded, or lost.

Because to be human is to get what you want
that leaves you with more want,

the dogs are laughing
at something nearer: the painter, how little pleasure
he takes from the moon, colors, dogs.

BECAUSE APRIL WAS A CRUEL MONTH

in a cruel year I switched from a gluten-free
to an all-gluten diet,
and God help me

if eating can't be about pleasure in these times
—*O carbs!*—
induce in me a dreamy state

as if back in Florence falling
cliché-in-love
with an Italian chef

who will become my husband,
back when he couldn't
hold back his tears

when I had to leave the Uffizi
—shortness of breath—

Stendhal syndrome, he said,
when I thought it was just dehydration,
since drinking

had become secondary
in the throes
of our joie de vivre,

back when he said *how lucky* to have scored
someone easily displaced
by beauty,

and I was naïve to declare appetite
our currency, sufficient and infinite.
In a pandemic,

marriage becomes a marathon we run indoors:
nights I feed
his obsession with wild yeast,

marvel there's food where there is air,
given only
water and flour, given time.

PORTRAIT, SEVEN YEARS AFTER

I know your face when you were hiding it
among the trees,
                    in the moon's halo,
inside the frost.

You listen to a pot of rice because it sings
to say it's done.

I walk past midnight to watch the theater
of windows and lights,

heart thickened by solitude,
in the morning you wake me

sun-facing,   our room
                        bloomed
libidinal. We still vow
to wave all
        other loves close.

Sometimes we are arid, sometimes
a rainforest. Sometimes

we are empty,
as in the beginning.

Your name
        which means sunlight opened mine,
which means wound.

AUTOBIOGRAPHY

I was the first of the C-sections
        and the first word I learned was *sorry*.
                Every time I looked at my mother

I was overwhelmed to sleep.
        The lives of ants took grip: I too,
                wanted to be led by smell,

and if be finished, be finished
        by a burning slant of light.
                If there were to be an inheritance,

it would be *siesta*. The hour
        when we praised
                what we found along the horizontal.

To hear the unspoken, I learned
        in three languages: *sorry, sorry, sorry*.
                I spilled my mother's Spanish perfume

and lied about it. I still wanted
        to be loved in ways that were considered
                healthy. At present a scent

like that of a conqueror's cloak
          cannot be scrubbed out between us.
                    To be a daughter is to discipline

oneself to only want the chalk
          taste of *gumamela*,
                    thoughts all lungfish breathing

under water. Mother, the ants in the garbage
          hotel hump atop a grain of sugar.
                    When they disappear, the walls move.

OUR HANDS WILL NOT TOUCH

in the dough bowl, so when my mother phoned
        I said *knead longer not harder, then wait.*
This advice confounds her,

how to let time do
        what hands cannot. I should have said
this is the logic of yeast, the invisible work

of growth. I should have said *fire*
        needs air. Who hasn't craved
for the pandesal of her young motherhood,

of nights long hospital shifts
        in the big city, a fullness I imagined
she was having without me, pork pineapple stews

to be soaked by the rolls
        more sweet than salt,
dusted with days-old crumbs:

she always arranged them on the plate like a bed
        of brown pebbles offering comfort.
Because even then I could count

how many times my mother's hands
            and mine had touched, I listened
to her new passion for cooking

with a weariness
            children reserve for adults.
After her call I looked up kairos again,

because of a recent movie I saw with a friend.
            Here is the asymmetry I still
cannot resolve. How I met my friend for tea,

years before my mother's call. How we laughed
            about my dating life, that once,
when the sheets got busy, I had to stop because of the crucifix

necklace dancing above me. How it felt
            like I was having a threesome
with Jesus. But why this memory with this

more recent story, like some numen passing,
            some small golden place
at the intersection of guilt and abandonment?

DECEMBER

I want to give up my name,
become more

animal than
        woman, wanting warmth,
then more ancient

than dog. I miss the cold water
from the tap that I splash
                on my face

in the sinewy mornings, sitting the way
Siddhartha sat

under a fig tree,
           small poisons peeling
off me, and like this I come home
again:

        I massage the ground, foot by foot;
I run my hands down
        my lover's back,

feeling each bone, and he'd look up—
what is it
        to be touched thoroughly?

Come December let me want and do nothing.

When Mara demanded the Buddha *proof*
for who you think you are,
        so I too can say,

pressing down my palm: the earth,
only the earth
                is my witness.

FEEDING FIRE

I can't leave it alone,
the fire in the woodstove.

Not too much or the fire will starve,
                    return to stubborn wood and mock
your hurry to get away from the cold.

Which bark will give way the fastest
                    what does it need

Sit through it until you're sure there are no good fires
and no bad fires.   Bring the forest of self

for kindling and never throw in

everything at once—

It needs to be left alone completely to its future.

—log by log until
you can hear the song of ash.

is it hungry,

wants more paper

What are your reasons to start a fire?

the sound of flames,
the smoke of possibilities.

Light what resists burning:
a day made entirely of water, spiders

of thought that ran to get away
from the heat,

Ash, tell me, was it cedar
or birch or pine that burned?

PRE-DEPARTURE

You are going to a country
where you can have   a human shape

without being such.
 It's a simple enough

premise. Learn the phrase
a human is here, it means more

than your name.   You ask
is there anything
we can be but human?

This country is home
to forest   guardians,
     duendes,   shape
shifters.

Tao po: repeat it, accent
on the last syllable.

What you say, who you say it to,

opens doors: *tao po*.

You will announce   you're a person
outside   someone's gate,

what the visited   will hear
before   they let you in.

Our country   is a beauty mark
on the Pacific's cheek.

Everyone you'll meet
would have said it:
the dirt poor,   the dirt wealthy.

The paramilitary says it   then waits
for the targeted   to open their door.

Claim your tongue, no matter
how flawed.   You must

shape shift again,
again and again.

ELEGY FOR HACIENDA LUISITA

1.

I remember her bone-dry hands,
that she laughed at the police
when they threw farmers in jail,

how she taunted them to light her cigarette.
I remember we brought pots
of adobo and steamed rice.

It is tradition in the islands to offer food
to the grieving, and for them
to offer it back. Like this we partook

of her grief as we ate lunch together.
I remember she thanked us
for listening,   *so that one day, we can*

also help you.   I remember how open
the fields of sugarcane, how bald.
How I said sorry,
            how much larger

I needed to grow my heart to understand
her kind of freedom, that seeking
to give back to another person.

2.

Say *hacienda* and I imagine horses,
a mestizo riding through fields
of tobacco and sugarcane.

Chilled cane juice poured by the help.
Dusk, and the genteel sister poses

for a portrait inside the ancestral house,
lifts a gloved hand to her forehead
that shimmers into the present moment.

There are so many kinds of privilege.
Saying no to sugar is one.

Having enough months to fit
into a wispy dress
for a wedding in a wine-country ranch.

3.

A hacienda is not a ranch. From the Spanish *hacer*: to make,
as in to make the land productive.

When I get stuck, a monk tells me to sit still for a while, to let
the soil in me lie fallow.

A monk's wisdom tells me if we wait long enough,
land transforms into food,

the dead giving way to the living.

The present moment is this: sugarcane farmers in Hacienda Luisita
earn less than a dollar a week.

When they formed a picket line to protest their hunger, the military
fired and killed seven, then arrested dozens. The hacenderos, members
of the President's family.

In our homeland, we stay up with the dead. The dead
rowed away on a boat,
like this
    our hands work beyond death.

4.

I don't know a lot of facts.
                     My hands don't know
          what to do with them.
I aspired to catalogue different kinds of poverty.
                     I could only be sure of mine.
Farmers dug hands into dirt,
turned it over.
This was their protest.
            As their hands dug into dirt,
broke open the dead,
what should I have done with my hands,
          my dead?
         What good is my empathy
if it crumbles when touched?
Circling back, over and over, as if what I want
                  is a shore on the next island.

5.

I had been wandering into privilege's spacious rooms
freshened with purified air,

brightened by spilled sunlight.

It is privilege to come home and be told that trauma
gets lodged in the body.

How to witness, how to release. It is privilege to come home.

Here the cartoon my family drew,
me with superpowers prevailing over my sweet tooth.

The Tagalog word for resist is prefaced
by *pakiki*— join in—

because no one rises up alone,

because the act entangles the self.

ALL OF US ARE CLEAVED,

but only some are winged,
and from the sky we can tell
where the fire started,

where the bodies are buried,
how the mountain crumbled,
cities where children still run,

alone, unafraid, uncaged,
headlong to their families
who we called dreamers.

We must only stay awake:
what fuels flight is muscle
and memory.

GOOD AMERICANS

April 2020

The mayor says we're all in this together. And Asian Americans
more than ever, only need to be the best Americans.

Hard-headed parents: mine casino-hopped,
did as they pleased like real Americans,

whose streets are swept safe, whose slurs fall like sparks
on my masked sisters tending to Americans,

while coyotes roam San Francisco at night.
Imagine these lands unpeopled, empty of Americans.

Undocumented farmers, food workers, most essential:
a country separates you from exceptional Americans

armed to be happy, to be released back
to their money, who want to shop, be good Americans.

If I say our inhales are braided to their exhales,
is that un-American?

Invisible virus, we rapture and rage. You rupture us whole.
I live in contradictions, while American.

I GO TO THE OCEAN TO LEARN ABOUT DISTANCE,

the Pacific crashing,
the delight of dogs
for whom waves
            mean play,

the virus now jumping
across bodies,
morning buses all over

the world   near empty.
Must I always feel abandoned?

The questions
are always questions
of belonging.

I clan with the canine who had cut a swath
on the bed,
espresso-colored and ocean-salted.

How far is everyone else now
or should be.

Long ago on a California1AX bus,
we were near
and far at once.

I would count the faces
bowed over altars of flickering lights:

to look was the only prayer
I could offer.   Dear God

I know I was one of them too—

prayers thrown to the waves,
words of a lapsed Catholic,

a faltering Buddhist, pawing at language,

the water trying
to answer back.

I SEEK THE GHOSTS FIRST

and when they come I will build a house so I can live
with them. How do I stay

present when my present extends ten years forward,
twenty years back?

Time is a line, yes, and also a swirl?

The ghosts laugh. We measure time
not as something to spend,

but something to thicken and taste.

What is this year but a boot camp to learn how to leave
things unfinished,

how to let the invisible take a turn.

I say boot camp but I mean house.

I'm assigned to cut the carrots,
the momentum of my hands marching

to slice them into thick, orange coins. Can I make
a difference by doing nothing

as peaceably as I can?

If I love my neighbors, can I stand their silence?

How else to say success
beyond saying we've nailed it?

Someone start the conversation (I wrote

conversion), I promise I will follow.

I admit I still want
to finish my job with the vegetables, my want

as big as violence. I want them
all on a pile, measured, tidied, maimed:

normal has been pursuing me all my life

in the old right side up.

ARE YOU BRINGING FRUITS, PLANTS, SEEDS,

animals, disease agents,
snails?
          soil?   O border

agent,   buffed and blushing,
monsters
          are portable too.   The one Hollywood
imported,   the one wild and winged
and cleaved
          at the waist?   She would travel
her tendriled   tongue
across   your stone wall abs   to reach

the soft liver,   her hunger   a murder.

What is the value
          of all the articles   that will remain
               in the United States?

I must have heard you say
          particles, which is only partly
what we are,

                 since we are also waves,
       reporting   back to the moon.   Forgive me,

I must have been daydreaming   of pounded rice
                 sweetened   with crab fat.
I am looking at you   and thinking fondly

            of red,   necessary agent
to other colors.   It's 5:40 AM, we are both hungry

and my advice is bread.   Do you know a rosebud
that refuses
            to bloom is called a bullet?   How many flowers now

spangle our streets, dear agent, because our country
is a clenched fist?

Step in front of the camera   *try*
           not to smile   O but I have
more to declare.

BREAKING WATER

Much grows in mud
                    not in spite of mud,
and I'm making a life   out of my little failures.

Stepmom has something hopeful about it,
but although I'm a step
I don't think
I'm a mom. I did buy
       into the therapist's advice,

to think of myself as a bonus
mom.

Bonus as in optional, right, like in a quiz?

I always give extra items to make sure
the kids do good. They say
I'm an easy A.

My biology was the topic: the therapist asked
what about you.   I said there are enough

things to birth and mother
in this world.   My task was to let myself believe it.

First step: give a hundred dollars a month
for drinking water in Africa,
because the charity's millennial founder said

water is the only binary thing left
in the world,

and I fell in love with this idea.

How else to get clear choices
but to measure what is potable or not.

Some grieved the village girls
                    who took their lives after breaking

the water jars miles from their homes.
It was their mothers I couldn't forget,
having lost
what's precious twice.

I must have been feeling the opposite,
a grief for what didn't exist.

If I can't name what's lost how
can I emerge from mourning?

When I see the village cut the ribbon
to a new water well

I let myself be rinsed in their unambiguous joy.

YOU ASK FOR POETRY,

but I can only offer

the meadow between   yep   and   rot.

Our freedom comes
                from being fed more.

Some days our marriage
                is a grim area.

In our growing soft towards the middle,

our appetite,   late at night,
                is no more than a peep tit,

my beloved,   my bold,

my eve.

AUTOBIOGRAPHY

I come from long years of clothes strung
on a line,   sun bleached,
from humid hands,
                              from a long line of women
who hover too much and then not at all,

from children as afterthought,

a thin sliver of a chapter on hope,

small bodies meant for labor.   I come from the rubber
capital of the world. I had picked the explosion

of orange jungle geraniums each morning, beat
the bees and birds

to the sugary lick, the leaked light

I recognized as precious, as wild animals do,
its name *santan* in Tagalog:

              how I love a word with proximity to saint and devil

depending on the tongue,
also to the sun, how it taught me

that the left behind was what needed tending.

POEM WITH MIGRATION AND SPIDERS

They teach about exposure,
how to posture the abdomen
towards the sky, repurpose it

with silk. They know home is
anywhere gossamer and juice,
low flying clouds can float

them away towards new lands
with untapped resources.
They only needed to catch on

the right amount of wind,
let it carry them and their treasures
with it, preferably a breeze.

EMERGENCY MATINS

Summon now   the mourners
the rice farmers   the indigenous

Bodies   in bathtubs   in ditches
in other bodies   we bring you
our salves our lauds

Let mother break away   from smother
Coax the persimmons   into the sweetest snow

I want to be like spiders   who know
it's early enough to extrude
gossamer clouds   in peace

I want the poets to petition the gods for our future
to say there is laughter
              inside our slaughter
we are all just   foraging in the dark

And from your walled garden   O tyrant
send nothing   receive no one
to carry out your sentences

Let the healers come   we are falling
and there is no ground

I turn   towards the sun

In our fields of grief   poppies
profligate   unclench

HOMETOWN

Your green creates in me a craving for sour.

I miss your cool and storied dark
like cave mouths,
a house in the middle of a field,

a single fluorescence and a woman sorting
out rice grains from stones.

I long for your dark at the edge

when I've lived too long
in polished cities, among the overly bright.

Sometimes when someone speaks,
some dark is let out,
all amnion and possibility.

Will you see me through this thirst for salt and mud,

tell fire to lick her lips, be satisfied
she has eaten enough?

GIRL UNDER RIVER

what girl turns   away
from   cake   the stampede
of cousins

towards the mountains
and creature

she must ask permission from
stepping into   their soil

blessed   cursed   fertile
blossoming and eating
her fears

oh the sweetness
of the air up there
in the mouths of caves

a life   undercurrent   like an eye
swimming   up against
a gelatinous river

no matter how bright
half the story belongs to her
dark body

ORIGIN STORY

The water has come and that is its business.
We immersed
                  then rose from the water.

Look, we said, our country

is a jigsaw puzzle   bobbing up and down the water.

Let the children scatter the pieces
                         all over the water,
keep the water inside sacred
                          and the water outside aspirational.
The ocean
owns nobody. No one writes borders
                in the ocean,

caulks nations, says all the water.

We are buoyant because water seeks to join water,
like attracts like.

What we want is paper to send letters to

once-lands,

to say the water where we began
                    is the water that calls us back.

SMALL ACTS OF RESISTANCE: TALKING BACK TO OFFICIAL FORMS

Have you thought about the "official" documents we use regularly? They ensure we are participating as "good" consumers and "law-abiding" citizens; or they gatekeep our claim to the spaces we inhabit. On one hand they are some of the most unpoetic, uninspired documents around. Yet when met with the spirit of inquiry and curiosity, some humor and resistance, they offer new opportunities to re-imagine our beliefs and roles in our communities, as well as interrogate the limitations they place upon us.

In the past, when I used to travel with a Philippine passport, my re-entries to the U.S. were often met with acute scrutiny and sometimes distrust. Immigrants and foreign visitors know to deploy a polite and skillfully-crafted acquiescence. In some poems in this collection, I imagine what it must be like if the conversations in these transit points were more complex, instead of purely transactional. What does agency in these situations look and feel like?

PROMPT:

Look at some of the documents lying around your house or office: tax returns, oath of citizenship, voter guides, passports, credit card applications, birth certificates, bus & plane tickets, immigration & customs declaration' forms, etc. Underline some phrases you find charged, odd or interesting. On a separate piece of paper, do something totally different: write a favorite line from a poem, song or proverb or a new scientific fact you learned; or an idea about yourself or your community you've been grappling with. You can also look through your notebook for lines, words or images you are trying to find a poem for. From these free writes, craft a response to the "official" language you found. The leaps your mind will make might surprise you.

REPRESENTATIVE POEMS:

Gratitude Journal" (p. 2)
Pre-departure" (p. 18)
Are you bringing fruits, plants, seeds," (p. 31)

CATALOGUES AND SELF-PORTAITS

I love the Buddhist notion of "dependent co-arising." Simply stated, it posits that we are all simultaneously creating each other. It touches on our deep interdependence. In my introduction, I mentioned how skeptical I feel about "identity," about the descriptors and definitions that can be attributed back to a person. I always feel that the self unfolds and is revealed more truthfully in the encounters and objects one pays attention to, in the lists one makes, in the activities one chooses to do & in the people one loves and belongs to. On a related note, this is perhaps why I feel that when I write ekphrastic poems, more often than not, they also become self-portrait poems.

PROMPT:

Stand or sit in the middle of your room, garden, kitchen or work-space. Take note of all the objects that you keep trying to tidy up and put away—letters, broken plates, stones. Pay special attention to the stubborn ones: those you cannot quite control, like invasive grass or a pile of used books. What words & emotions do you connect with these objects? What narrative about yourself or identity is revealed by them? Craft an ode, a self-portrait poem, or a list poem

REPRESENTATIVE POEMS:

"Self-portrait as Heap & Wilt" (p. 1)
"Adult Swim Class" (p. 4)
"Portrait, Seven Years After" (p. 8)
"Tamayo's *Animales*" (p. 5)
"Autobiography" (pp. 10)

THE QUESTIONS WE CARRY,

the ones that usually cannot be answered, are the ones that carry us *forward* and bring us to new places in our imagination. In our writing and poetic practice, questions can efficiently interrupt declaratives and disrupt established stories. On the level of craft, whenever I feel stuck or when I feel that I have defaulted into my usual habits of writing and thinking, I take a sentence and see if it gains energy when posed as a question. I believe that deeply felt questions jolt us awake, and that infusions of doubt can lead to more interesting discoveries and poems.

PROMPT:

Take an existing poem draft or journal entry and look closely at your phrases or sentences. Is there a place that can pivot or go to a new direction if you interrupt your thought with a question? Alternatively, make a list of all the questions you carry, from the most mundane to the most profound. See if some of these questions can find a home in a poem.

REPRESENTATIVE POEMS:

"Our hands will not touch" (p. 12)
"I go to the ocean to learn about distance" (p. #27)
"I seek the ghosts first" (p. 29)
Are you bringing fruits, plants, seeds," (p. 31)
"Breaking Water" (p. 33)

ACKNOWLEDGMENTS

I am grateful to the following publications where these poems first appeared, often in slightly different and earlier versions:

Literary Mama: "Breaking Water"
MiGoZine: "I go to the ocean to learn about distance," "I seek the ghosts first," and "Good Americans"
Pedestal Review: "Gratitude Journal
RHINO: "Tamayo's Animales," and "*Are you bringing fruits, plants, seeds,*"
SFPL Poem-A-Day: "Pre-departure"
Spoon River Poetry Review: "Self Portrait as heap and wilt,"
The Global South: "Elegy for Hacienda Luisita"
Written Here & There, 2020: "Emergency Matins"

"All of Us Are Cleaved" is inspired by a line from Filipino writer Ricky Lee, in his novel *Si Amapola sa 65 na Kabanata*: "Lahat tayo hati, hindi nga lang nakakalipad ang iba."

"Emergency Matins" borrows phrases and devices from the poems in Dilruba Ahmed's *Bring Now the Angels* and Ocean Vuong's *On Earth We Are Briefly Gorgeous.*

Thank you to RHINO Founders' Prize 2022 and contest judge Luisa A. Igloria for choosing "*Are you bringing fruits, plants, seeds,*" to receive this honor.

Gratitude to poets & friends who gave space to and helped shape many of these poems: Joi Barrios, Aileen Cassinetto, Lourdes Figueroa, Yeva Johnson, Tehmina Khan, María Gómez de León, Lydia Liu, Christina Lloyd, Abigail Licad, Beatriz Yanes Martinez, Florencia Milito, Rachel Myers, Therí Pickens, Mark Prudowsky, Amy Shimshon-Santo, Angela Siew, Shradha Shah, Karen Terrey, Angela Torres.

Thank you to the communities in Hedgebrook, Community of Writers, The Grind and the Warren Wilson College MFA Alumni who continue to encourage poems and poets. Thank you to the Filipnx faculty, alumni, staff and student community at UC Berkeley for the shared vision & solidarity towards a more just & inclusive world. To the Philippine American Writers and Artists (PAWA) & Filbookfest for the collaborations & literary friendships. Deep appreciation to Nomadic Press especially to J. K. Fowler, for creating an empowering space for multitudes of voices, and to poet and editor Karthik Sethuraman, who helped make this collection stronger.

Love to my family, my father & mother, Romeo & Celia, my sisters Sharon & Rocelle, and nephew and niece Audrey & Roqo.

For my husband Bruno Soleri, whose passion, love & sensibility propel me forward. Thank you for asking to read the early drafts. Thank you for the feast that is our shared life and home, for Lorenzo, and for our boddhisatva dogs, Boccia & Oso.

I dedicate this book to Dr. Avelina T. Llagas (1930-2021): what a miraculous gift that you were my *lola*.

KAREN LLAGAS

Karen Llagas's first collection of poetry, *Archipelago Dust*, was published by Meritage Press in 2010. A recipient of a RHINO Founder's Prize, Filamore Tabios, Sr. Memorial Poetry Prize and a Hedgebrook residency, her poems and reviews have also appeared in various journals and anthologies. Born and raised in the Philippines, she lectures at UC Berkeley, and currently divides her time between San Francisco and Los Angeles. More about her at www.karenllagas.com

Printed in the USA
CPSIA information can be obtained
at www.ICGtesting.com
CBHW030703060224
4083CB00003B/2

9 781955 239431